WHERE THE TRUTH LIES

poems by

Kerry O'Keefe

Finishing Line Press
Georgetown, Kentucky

WHERE THE TRUTH LIES

ACKNOWLEDGMENTS

"Where The Truth Lies," "Crone," "Ten O'Clock," "Jack, "Our Good Divorce,"
and "Parking Lot Haiku" appeared in the winter 2009-2010 edition of March
Street Press' journal, *Parting Gifts*.
"Hometown" appeared in the Fall 2015 edition of the *Naugatuck River
Review*

Editor: Christen Kincaid

Cover Art: Kerrigan Grace Canzano

Author Photo: Kerry O'Keefe

Cover Design: Elizabeth Maines

Printed in the USA on acid-free paper.
Order online: www.finishinglinepress.com
also available on amazon.com

Author inquiries and mail orders:
Finishing Line Press
P. O. Box 1626
Georgetown, Kentucky 40324
U. S. A.

Table of Contents

For my mother,
Jane Gamble O'Keefe

St. Paddy's Day, Third Generation

She cuts the plastic bag then dumps the corned beef
into the boiling water. Something pink and salty
splashes back. She thinks of the child she miscarried
twelve years ago, day after St. Paddy's. Of the son
she bore three years later on the feast day itself, a boy
who wishes he were Vito Corleone. But, *ah, the Irish*,
her mother would say with a boozy laugh,
As if just saying would excuse the story of an uncle
or father turned up hung over one more time on the Old Sod.
Wiring from Dublin to the wife in New Haven for the cash
to get home. Ah, the uproarious tales of drying out farms.
The piety of wives and the pleading. The well-
earned solace of the whores. Ah, the flayed hearts
of the little girls as they grew into tight-lipped women,
mute when it came to telling the rest of the story. Stingy
with their love. Doomed to the sheepish wearing of the green,
the yearly dropping of salted meat into brine.

Cleaning up the Myth

Across the street, the grave
of a neighbor's dead dog sparkles
brightly with the many lights
of Christmas. Power lines bristle
under ice as you skid drunkenly away,
head packed with big ideas, useful
as a mouth full of rotted teeth.
Left side of the bed cold and empty.
A the jug of vodka *someone* tossed
into the hedge. I lie awake and remember
our loving. Taking comfort in
the sound of the plows, wild boars
harnessed and butting against the snow.
Wrestling Mother Nature to one side.
Trying to make order out of the mess
so that maybe, goddammit, life can go on.

Big Sister Death

Remember, it is not just the cadaver
that gets to be glamorous. Dressed
finely in the indelicacy of her new
leisure, languishing in the capacity
to outwait everyone and lording
that lack of need over us all.
I say, forget the ten year old washer
as it rocked across the floor
with your mock silk blouse
thrown in with the terrycloth towels,
that frightening noise it makes
when overloaded. Let it be a memory
we don't repeat as you step out of the hearse
with the others. Just remember who
you are competing with, and what.
Show a little ankle. Lose with style.

Where The Truth Lies

Her last days escape like pennies, rolling
off the table. You know and she knows
and life is more beautiful for that. Her stubbornness
pungent as raw ginger. Her eyes seek the floor
and the line of her mouth tightens as
the doctor gently says there is no hope. "So,"
finally she says, "what about this constipation?"
Color drains from the doctor's face and for once
you keep quiet. Let her have this will that once
almost crushed you. And after, on the ride home,
just as disbelieving sorrow starts to fill the car
she speaks again. "Look at those clouds," she says.
Conversational, as if you were once again a child
in the back seat and she were young at the wheel.
Again you let her lead, and indeed you both peer up
at these great bustles of white fabricated in an endless
brilliant sky, overlooking everything.

Crone

I have a small room with a floor painted coral.
An ex-lover who says he hates my guts, even
after borrowing my heart all these years—saying
he liked the loud sound it made when he shook it.
I have the laughter of the girls visiting the boys
in the three quarter house across the lot.
The sound of their tv through the screen door
makes my late afternoons important. I still
have at least half my beauty, starting to hang
a little off my cheekbones, but nonetheless. I hoard
a humble portion of faith in a god whose shape
changes daily, some days, draped in a white cloth,
other days, red lips and a husky voice that issues
from the depths of the sea. Every once in a while, God
takes off its clothes and just feels around inside my chest.
I have silence at the end of the day as it lowers onto my bed,
after the years of clamor and tugging of children and
the men. Silence, in waves, in choruses. Streaming,
stewing, rubbing me down like a mother drying her child
after the tub. Holding me tightly between it's sturdy knees
while I look around, disarmed and bemused. Who knew?

The Heart's Fine Bungling

I can only thrash my way back into our story.
Trying to resuscitate the details of the love.
Pure, shining moments strung like tiny seed pearls
between big red flares of defeat. We've managed
this thing like emergency workers on ecstasy.
Always grabbing the wrong colored flag.
Sending the ambulance over to put out the fire.
Turning the hose on the woman giving birth.
Handing out doughnuts to the shocked and grieving
at the roadside wreck. Coming home, flipping on
the tube - it would have made too much sense to weep.

Ten O'Clock

It is ten o'clock and each number you press
leads you away from the life you have known.
Not your husband's name you speak into the phone,
out in the darkened parking lot of the mall.
Asking if the hour is too late. Letting him listen
to you bubble on about lipstick and the sales.
Yet even under the riot of your blood, you begin to feel
the numbness of one watching a distant avalanche.
How grandly it all begins to crumble.
Now that there is no talk of coincidence.
No lying about business or chance.
Nothing in this phone call but desire,
one last bird setting down in the dark snow.
The roar of everything falling after that.

Jack

When I was young, wild was all about
Jack Daniels. The night I walked
into a ditch and Charlie and T.C.
had to pour bourbon all over my knee.
After that, we kept on drinking until the sun
poured itself on us. Then we could safely
go home, each alone. Drunk and victorious
at another night spent covering up
our desire. Youth is time spent confusing
what is agitation with what is wild.
And then I found myself, forty-five
waking, cold sober, in Jack's bed, with
the light pouring in past the whiteness
of him working at his desk. My children
in another town, my marriage dismantled.
My memory pure and intact as my will.
The future a mystery. My heart, full
and severe. Wild is what he found
when he put his pen down and came over.

Good Friday, 2008

Winter geese scatter as a door slams.
Naked trees usher in the hope of bursting open
in the name of the Lord. Hallowed
be the name of the missing. The sea
out from under slush—seaweed stuck
to a stone, the fisherman's dream. Gather
the folds, wipe that face, and wipe it again
'til it shines. Enter the wind then the white calm
of a stone. Follow those tracks left in the sand,
from the smell of fish to the smell of fish frying.

Striptease

The first layer to go, toss the jacket over the chair,
shirt onto the desk over the letters and bills.
Let the skirt slowly fall to the floor as I allow the children's
soccer schedule slowly to fade from the live bibliography
of my mind. Bra on the bedside table, stranded on a stack
of self-help books with their guilty layer of dust.
Last item to go, threadbare black cotton
bikini from the Gap, hurled to its fate where the mattress
meets the top sheet down in the corner of my side of the bed.
Now lay your cheek on my chest and hear what pounds up
with the gray persistence of high tide in December.
Come inside and tell me you know
exactly what I am thinking.

Our Good Divorce
For Ed

Love like the apple tree out back,
not expected to survive the man
who came one day with a saw, started
at the top and worked his way down.
Nothing left but the trunk, half-dead,
and a single branch. Who could have
predicted the blossoms that spring?
In fall, the handful of apples?

Any God

We take our fathers' bright inconsistencies and cruelties,
the empty wide boulevard of his need, and drape those
qualities like a serape over the broad shoulders of God.
The cool gaze our mothers' aimed each morning past
the corner of our ears as she waited to be left alone.
They chose against us, tried to stop us, or simply forgot.
We are certain God is made in their image, those who
molded the hearts we bring to prayer. Hearts so lacquered
with fury or grief, they embody an unspeakable calm.
Offered to a god whose face we may never recognize.
"Here," we say, nonetheless, with our strange way
of begging, "Save this."

Parking Lot Haiku

snow on the windshield
fresh jeans folded in a bag
soon, visiting hours

Not Love

Not love, they fell in step
like two bears in a blizzard
Asking, what is love but an idea
that cannot be eaten? More than lovers
they become two noses, two sets of jaws
against the adversaries. One shared
roar alerting offspring of danger
or food. Together, staring at the moon
in rare moments of repose. Asking
what is love but the name
someone from a distance gives
the fierce throttle of muscle and fur
arranging the darkness before
the silence of a vigilant sleep.

Hometown

The Lord is all that's left of my hometown.
Everyone else dead or drunk beyond recognition.
or old, like me. I barely recognize myself,
handsomely grey and sick to death
of snow in winter, Stevie Wonder
and the Brandenburg Concertos.
With some alarm, I find myself envying
the men under the bridge, houseless
but good at making any sidewalk home.
Thank God for the Lord, willing to talk to me
as I wander through this now childless edifice,
unable to sit for too long, He will follow me
into the bathroom, chatting while I shower.
Reminding me of the smell of my mother's
Irish American version of eggplant parmigian'.
The way the beach looked on Christmas Day.
The Lord remembers the bad parts as well,
but is a gentleman, and lets me be the one
to bring them up. Sometimes I look into his eyes
and see my old street name: Neptune. Sometimes
if we stand together quietly, I can coax him
into loaning me back the feeling I used to have
on Sundays at St. Margaret's. My father home in bed
but sober. The altar before the wood changed
to chrome. Hymns and Latin responses offered freely
tumbling out of my mouth with no thought of return.

Mukhtaran Bibi

I want to know was each man who raped her
alone in the room or did he do it
in front of the others? Were his trousers around his ankles
or was his robe held high above his waist?
Did he leave his sandals on? Was his mother still alive
and if so, was she proud of him that day? What
was he thinking as he wiped her blood
and the scum of the man before him off.
Wasn't he just a little afraid? And what did he eat
for dinner that night? Which worlds between him
and his wife as he lay down beside her
pungent with the scent of another woman
and the men? Would he have noticed
the way from that day on, his wife changed?
The rich excitement of village life with its
stonings and amputations.
Now and then a hanging, yet how often
was there fortune enough to congregate
in the occasion of actual sex? How intent
was their listening? Very intent.
How could they explain how it felt, the sense
of dark justice and the tingling. The final insult,
village children in the crowd watching as the woman
emerged, not permitted enough to fully cover
herself as she walked the shock of her body home
to where it would only be decent to die.
The men linger, shaking their heads as the women
go home to cook. Each of them undefended
and weak; unprepared in any way for the fact
that the woman would choose her life.

Speak in a voice that would transverse continents.
Build the school for the boys, the school for the girls.
seeming to thrive in plain daylight, in the twilight,
the marketplace, the square
where any decent villager could see.

Early Winter

Drugs have made an exile of my son.
Soccer shoes and a sweatshirt
All that is let of him in the hall.
My daughter with her strawberry curls
drives herself to school. Men
who once had houses and plane tickets, write
and call, saying *we must look after each other*
which means they are running out of cash.
This body has become a lean, salt-beaten cottage
on a dune. I move slowly
around my room. Make the bed. Put a match
to a fleck of sage in an ashtray once owned
by my mother. I stoop to pick up
a dime. Listen to the bird in the next yard,
this late November. Unlike me
she seems unconcerned,
singing loudly, and for pleasure.

Before Finding Out About Happiness

If Aphrodite were to ask me, I would have to answer
a question with a question. About that night at the stoplight
on Sisson at 2:30 a.m. across from the tuxedo rental shop,
and everything that followed. My prayer to be put in a different
city—or to have him go, knowing it was a question of my life.
As it turned out, alcohol got taken away instead. Which left the man
but after that it didn't matter since for a while I was afraid of
    everything,
stuck as I was with a wad of frozen scar tissue that would have
to function as a heart. Where was Aphrodite that year, or the year
after that? By now Davy would have left me for Carol.
Jack was still unknown, but soon Tim would be making jokes
about throwing me down the stairs. Clearly, all that could be done
was more waiting in the gray, soggy air of Hartford. Maybe
Aphrodite would call those years exercise. Stretching and
    limbering.
Preparation. Getting the blood flowing again after a bad beginning.
Rehearsal maybe, or just plain passing the time. To which I might
    reply,
it was nearly half a lifetime, and while we were on the subject
I would tell her that her mysteries are stern, and as far as I knew,
her mercies invisible. But all that was before finding out about
    happiness.
Damned lucky to have never had the conversation with her at all.

Communion

Tonight it is the little girl in the film
who wakes me up. The dullness
in her eye as she lets her auntie know
about the moneyed uncle and his kisses.
A dinginess has taken over her spirit.
Which clarifies the mystery
of those pale Sundays I forced myself
out of bed to stand at the altar.
Banking on the blindness of the Lord.
Peaceful for a moment on the carpet,
near the gold.   Mouth and palms open.
I was shining.

Mythic

I come down early before children.
Try to measure my step and right away
slow down enough to think what I mean.
It is difficult.
Some days, the joy of putting grapes
or cashews in plastic bags,
then carefully taping them shut.
Dropping bacon into the pan.
Meaning to stay distinct from everything.
When I fail it is hard not to think
of something crumpled.
I have gone too long as I am.
And marvel at the woman who knows
a kind of importance she carries
by virtue of walking into a room.
I know it sometimes.

R.

a clear crystal glass
his finger tracing the rim
all night, the ringing

Meanwhile, The Body

The camera has captured the eyes of the moose
as it understands about the three wolves
not far behind. Its dark eyes stained
with a dignified sorrow one split second
before its body will respond. The spirit
knows better, moving slowly toward
the large piece of quiet which death is. Leaving
muscle and bone to gallop and thrash, able to think
only in units of gristle. The body
ready to break its own legs running. Before
the succulent quiet of the wolves as they feed.

In Bayonne

There was a time I
was a tall drink of water.
Some said in a former life
I had blood. Before my soul
leaked out of its paper cup all over
the floor of someone's back seat
and was gone. Even so
in Bayonne, I was the smell
of mint in the wall, the only cricket
to make it though your screen.
Keeping you safe and secure all night
with my explanations. Why, after all
did you come at me
brandishing your shoe?

Motherhood

I have halved myself and then some.
Settled once for stitches, brought the next one forth without.
Washed and rinsed backsides. Soaped heads.
Fashioned ditties dull enough to introduce sleep.
Plucked gum, lice and pieces of leaf
from long and short locks of sun and wind blown hair.
Held heads over baskets and bowls,
pressured napes and temples to blot out pain.
Breathed the pungence of sneakers in summer,
shook the stale sand, dumped the thermos of camp water
dead since noon. I have shaken the towels. Driven
the slouching sullen miles to school, pulled
the socks right side out. Dredged
forgotten, half-liquid sandwiches out of the pack.
Stashed the last nearly finished reading log
in the box where such items are kept for posterity.
Found the final "fuck" carved at the corner
of the very last headboard. I have weathered
all forms of complaint and have made my apologies.
Said my farewells, falsely smiling and robust.
Now the silence newly thunders, drowning out
even the sound of the summer birds
as it grinds up and down
over the last traces of juice on the stair.

January

The moon preceded by snow.
Branches stark as an angel's brow—
All the richness of summer, reversed.
The new year, a switch twisted off the tree
in spite of the sap. Thrown in the river.
We'll see where it ends up.

Kerry O'Keefe grew up on the Long Island Sound in Connecticut and received a B.A. from Trinity College. After a decade of singing blues, pop and jazz in the Hartford area, poems began to arrive. A first chapbook, *From A Burning Building,* was published by March Street Press. She was assisting in the preparation of Jack Gilbert's award-winning manuscript, *Refusing Heaven.* Journals which have published her poems include The Massachusetts Review, *canwehaveourballback, paragraph, Gris-Gris* and soon, *the Naugatuck River Review.* During her years in Western Massachusetts, she lead numerous ongoing writing workshops and was a member of the acclaimed critical workshop, Group 18. During this time, she wrote numerous interviews with Western Mass and Hudson Valley fine artists for the Berkshire artzine, *The Artful Mind.* Alternately writing poems, practicing Reiki, admiring her children and selling used cars, she currently lives outside of New York City. A town she adores.

9 781944 251918